Challenges to Freedom's March: Regional Democracy Trends and U.S. Foreign Policy

The Institute for the Study of Diplomacy (ISD), founded in 1978, is part of Georgetown University's Edmund A. Walsh School of Foreign Service and is the School's primary window on the world of the foreign affairs practitioner.

ISD studies the practitioner's craft : how diplomats and other foreign affairs professionals succeed and the lessons to be learned from their successes and failures. Institute programs focus on the foreign policy process: how decisions are made and implemented.

ISD conducts its programs through a small staff and resident and nonresident "associates." Associates, primarily U.S. and foreign government officials, are detailed to or affiliated with the Institute for a year or more. The Institute seeks to build academic-practitioner collaborations around issues using associates and Georgetown faculty. ISD staff and associates teach courses, organize lectures and discussions, mentor students, and participate on university committees.

In addition, ISD's Pew Case Studies in International Affairs are used in over 1,000 courses across the country and around the world.

Challenges to Freedom's March: Regional Democracy Trends and U.S. Foreign Policy

Sara E. Thannhauser

A Schlesinger Working Group Project
Institute for the Study of Diplomacy
Edmund A. Walsh School of Foreign Service
GEORGETOWN UNIVERSITY

Note: The views expressed in this report do not necessarily reflect the views of any of the organizations, governmental or private, with which the individual participants in the discussion group are affiliated.

Institute for the Study of Diplomacy
Edmund A. Walsh School of Foreign Service
Georgetown University, Washington, D.C.   20057–1025
© 2006 by the Institute for the Study of Diplomacy.

ISBN 0-934742-98-7
Printed in the United States of America

Contents

3
Southeast Asia's Democratic Challenge: Strength (and Weakness) in Diversity   37

Whither Democracy Promotion?   51

Schlesinger Working Group Core Members   61

About the Author   62

Acknowledgments

The Institute for the Study of Diplomacy (ISD) of Georgetown University established the Schlesinger Working Group in 1999. This program recognizes the distinguished public career of Dr. James R. Schlesinger and his remarkable contributions to national security policymaking and strategic thought. The Schlesinger Working Group is based on a multi-year working group initiative with a mandate to review and assess a range of possible scenarios that contain significant potentials for strategic surprises and for unanticipated outcomes. The Schlesinger Working Group relies on a permanent core membership of generalists from the policy-making and research communities and academia who are sometimes joined by respected authorities on specific regional or functional topics under consideration. The meetings are chaired by Schlesinger Professor of Strategic Studies Dr. Chester A. Crocker and ISD Director Professor Casimir A. Yost.

The Schlesinger Working Group extends a special thanks to those core members and guest presenters whose opening remarks laid the groundwork for the series' discussion. The group would also like to thank all guest participants who contributed both their highly relevant experience and their personal perspectives to the overall discussion.

Executive Summary

Speaking in his weekly radio address on March 5, 2005, President Bush proclaimed that "the trend is clear: in the Middle East and throughout the world, freedom is on the march." He pointed to the so-called "rainbow revolutions" in Lebanon, Georgia, and Ukraine, as well as to the democratic progress made in Afghanistan and post-Saddam Iraq as examples of this trend. Inspired by the president's proclamation, the Schlesinger Working Group embarked on a year-long series that examined the status of democratic trends in Latin America, Africa, and Southeast Asia, with a final discussion focused on U.S. democracy promotion and Middle East democracy trends.

For the past three decades, democracy has thrived on a global scale. In 1975, only 25 percent of the countries in the world were designated as "free." In 2005, 46 percent of the world's countries were classified as "free," and 122 countries out of 192 were classified as "electoral democracies."[1] Given these numbers, analysts suggest that democratic governance has become an established international norm over the last twenty-five years. Despite democracy's solid record of advancement, the Working Group Series identified formidable challenges that threaten democratic expansion throughout the world. In the first three meetings, participants uncovered regional obstacles

---

1. See Arch Puddington, "Freedom in the World: Middle East Progress Amid Global Gains," *Freedom House* (Washington, DC), http://65.110.85.181/upload/pdf/essay2006.pdf. It should be noted that Freedom House considers the term "electoral democracy" to be a minimal standard.

that hinder democratic consolidation in Latin America, Africa, and Southeast Asia.

All three regions continue to suffer from weak institutions, underdeveloped political party structures, limits on opposition movements, corruption, and, in some cases, popular demagoguery. In all three regions, the largest and most significant powers (Brazil, Nigeria, South Africa, and Indonesia) do not always wield their influence in a manner that positively affects the democratic development of their neighbors, nor is it certain that smaller democratic states have the ability to be regional democratic leaders. The three regions also share the risk of becoming "hijacked" democracies to the degree that (a) long-time incumbents and in some cases new arrivals (Hugo Chávez) are in a position to stack the political deck and manipulate electoral politicking; and/or (b) "people power" movements organize "the street" to force their will upon weak, elected governments that lose touch with their societies.

Group members also pointed out region-specific challenges. Economic trends differ substantially in each region. Socioeconomic inequality emerges as a critical and salient challenge with particular vehemence in Latin America. Incumbent leaders are subjected to the rigors of "performance legitimacy" tests to a greater extent in Southeast Asia and Latin America; African polities generally appear less respectful of term limits and more responsive to external donor pressures than to the demands of their own domestic societies. Africa's relative dependence makes it more vulnerable to western pro-democracy pressures, though this is declining due to Russian and Chinese willingness to support challengers to democratic norms. The "demonstration effect" of events in one country impacting trends elsewhere in the region is most pronounced in Latin America and Africa, but much less so in Southeast Asia due to differentiating and buffering circumstances. Southeast Asia and Africa still suffer from a substantial number of autocratic regimes. Fortunately, Latin America is home to only one true autocracy (Cuba).

The final meeting of the series addressed the status of the U.S. policy of democracy promotion, specifically examining U.S. perceptions of democracy, conditions under which the United States can successfully promote democracy, Middle East democracy dynamics, other regional challenges that inhibit democracy promotion, and potential surprise scenarios that may result in the reversal of democracy's positive global trend. During the meeting, Group members cautioned that the U.S.'s idealistic perception of democracy as a universal goal is not always shared, especially in regions such as Africa, Southeast Asia, and the Middle East. Democracy is often perceived by others more instrumentally as a tool to achieve objectives such as social justice or the redistribution of wealth and less as an intrinsically superior system of governance.

Another challenge to the U.S. policy of democracy promotion is knowing when, how, and where to engage in this effort. Participants generally doubted the effectiveness of using force to promote democracy. They also pointed out that promoting democracy in postconflict environments or inherently unstable or weak states can be problematic because of a lack of security. Moreover, it was noted that the U.S. government is not always the best vehicle to pursue democracy promotion, particularly in an era when U.S. policies are facing such widespread criticism.

During the final meeting, group members also considered some of the challenges to U.S. democracy promotion in the Middle East. There are many important changes taking place in the Middle East that may have little to do with U.S. democracy promotion efforts or rhetoric. Interestingly, these changes are often developing within the Islamist movement. According to one expert, Islamist parties are dividing themselves into religious and political organizations. The religious dimension is designed to appeal to the portion of their base that is committed to a certain set of values, while the political entity is designed to give the party the flexibility to be pragmatic enough to govern effectively. Some members argued that a certain degree of pluralism is forming in the Islamist movement. Like all political parties, the new Islamist parties will compete with each other and will have to perform in order to maintain influence.

Other group members were less optimistic. They contended that it is too early to determine whether or not these shifts are a sign of democratization. Furthermore, they drew pessimistic conclusions from the results of democratic elections held in Palestine, the recent events in Lebanon, the inability of the democratically elected Iraqi government to quell secular violence, and the prevailing number of entrenched autocracies present in the region.

There was also concern expressed regarding the rise of a palpable antidemocratic undertow at the multilateral level led by Russia and China. By aligning with other autocracies, both powers are pushing back and are threatening to gain influence on the issues of democracy, and governance standards and in opposition to external interference in national internal affairs. This development could emerge as the greatest potential strategic surprise identified by the Working Group's Series on democracy. Though this antidemocratic pole has yet to develop fully, it has gained enough momentum to threaten the global expansion and consolidation of democracy. Unless the United States is able to regain international credibility for enlarging democratic space, there is potential for a global retreat from the current preferential trend for democratic governance.

To address these challenges, participants concluded that democracy promotion should remain a priority in U.S. foreign policy. However, they argued that the present U.S. rhetoric and methods used to promote democracy fall short of the strategy required to deal with current challenges. A new strategy needs to be developed that looks through what are inevitably going to be unstable transitions and setbacks. Moreover, participants believed that fighting dictatorship and the antidemocratic backlash will require a subtle diplomatic hand. In some cases, pushing back hard may get results; in others, it may only fuel nationalist sentiments. The U.S. policy of democracy promotion must be consistent and patient. The United States must be mindful of the contradictions inherent in pressing for democratic changes in some countries and not in others and of pressing for elections and then questioning outcomes. Aid must be directed towards improving the homegrown institutional capacity programs, anticorruption initiatives, political pluralism forums, and human rights agendas in countries undergoing democratic transition and/or consolidation. Other group members contended that this strategy must also be legitimately seen as a multilateral endeavor, thereby neutralizing claims of authoritarian dictators that the policy is a unilateral U.S. project. To be successful against the sources of the democracy backlash, the United States must work with other democracies to coordinate their efforts to reclaim the initiative from Russia and China.

I

Latin America: Is Freedom Still On the March?

OVERVIEW

In the fall of 2005, the Schlesinger Working Group began a series of discussions focusing on democracy in Latin America, Africa, and Southeast Asia. The first meeting, which took place on November 22, 2005, discussed "Latin America: Is Freedom Still on the March?" Some observers suggested that while Washington pays significant attention to the challenge of democratization in the Arab world, democratic consolidation in parts of Latin America has become imperiled just one generation after authoritarian and military regimes disappeared from most of the region. The argument pointed to a combination of resurgent anti-Americanism, populist challenges to the Washington-consensus economic model,[2] antiglobalization, indigenous peoples' movements, and regional meddling by Hugo Chávez and Fidel Castro, which may result in a broader negative trend in hemispheric governance. The purpose of the meeting was to assess these claims as a regionwide phenomenon and also to explore what strategic surprises might be in store for the United States from Latin America. The group also examined policy recommendations to mitigate, avoid, or exploit these possible strategic surprises.

---

2. The Washington-consensus economic model is a policy the United States promoted in Latin America beginning in the 1980s that encourages open economies and capital flows, export-led trade, gross domestic product-measured growth, and "free" trade to combat poverty and inequality in the region.

I. SUMMARY

After much discussion, the working group remained divided on whether Latin America's commitment to democracy and free market principles is waning regionwide. Some participants suggested that there is no overall consensus in the region; its politics are fractured and fragmented. For instance, following the thorough demoralization of his opponents in the 2004 Venezuelan national referendum and subsequent local elections, Chávez continued to subvert democratic institutions. He is perceived to be using escalating oil wealth to challenge pro-American leaders in a number of other countries. Through his rhetoric and actions, Chávez is attempting to set a regional agenda in direct opposition to U.S. objectives. In a parallel development, in Ecuador, Peru, and Bolivia, indigenous political movements have gained strength, while they increasingly (and successfully) have used protest, blockades, and other tactics to challenge the overall legitimacy of the political order. They have also worked through the existing democratic systems to gain influence and representation.

Other participants believed that, though embattled in some countries, democracy and free market principles continue to enjoy widespread support and success in other countries. Chile has approved of globalization and implemented third-generation democratic reforms: transparency in governance, functioning institutions, and an allegiance to the rule of law. Colombia, under the leadership of Álvaro Uribe, has made significant strides in fighting against corruption, insurgent groups, and the illicit drug trade. Luiz Inácio "Lula" Da Silva, Brazil's president from the leftist Workers' Party, adheres to free market principles and is committed to democratic institutions. Furthermore, several participants pointed to the 2001 Quebec City Summit of the Americas, where regional leaders agreed to negotiate an Inter-American Democratic Charter, which was ratified on September 11, 2001, making democracy the only legitimate form of government in the Americas. Others underscored that leftist or indigenous challenges to representative government in some countries are paradoxically the result of greater participation and more inclusive democracy in these countries.

While the group was unable to determine whether the prospects for democracy in Latin America are seriously threatened, they were able to identify critical factors and forces that in combination could produce significant negative trends in the hemisphere. Though these factors are not strategic surprises in and of themselves—with the exception of Chávez—they can generate secondary effects that could produce startling results. Key challenges that face Latin America include the following:

- Widespread institutional incapacity and governance problems that delay the effective implementation of political, social, and economic reforms necessary to curb crime and enhance the legitimacy of democratic regimes;

- Corruption within political parties and ruling regimes, which causes a backlash and bolsters support for "antisystemic" populist movements;

- Inequality and exclusion of the poor and indigenous groups, exacerbated by the challenges of globalization (or, some suggested, due to the weakness of global trade and investment links in the region) and incomplete economic reforms;

- Weak states with porous borders, posing numerous threats in terms of terrorism and the illicit drug trade. Also, given the region's proximity to the United States, weak states that affect illegal immigration levels and contribute to the recycling of gang violence;

- A cacophony of anti-American rhetoric flowing from both leftist and rightist leaders in the region (antipathy is particularly directed toward the Bush administration); and

- Hugo Chávez's oil-financed populism and his success in morphing into a counterconsensus figure and potential political agenda setter for elites in places such as Argentina.

II. CHALLENGES FACING THE REGION

Institutional Incapacity

All participants agreed that Latin America suffers from major governance failures. Fragile government structures are ill equipped to manage regulatory frameworks and oversight mechanisms. A participant noted that a key expectation of a democratic state is the fair distribution of public goods and services. However, when democratic government structures fail in this regard, the legitimacy of these institutions is questioned, opening the door to competing political ideologies. For instance, in Bolivia, the unequal distribution of resources helped lead to an agitated political environment in which Evo Morales (a leftist indigenous leader) successfully took to the street with his platform that rejected the current governmental structure and public sector policies. Morales' ability to galvanize the myriad social movements representing the poor and the indigenous peoples propelled him to a resounding victory in Bolivia's election held on December 18, 2005. In addition to the poor and indigenous groups, he also drew support from many middle-class professionals and small entrepreneurs who overwhelmingly desired a change in Bolivia's traditional political institutions. With his victory, Morales now has a clear mandate for his program to nationalize the gas sector, convene an assembly to rewrite the constitution, expand the government, and enact land reform.

A critical regionwide effect of Latin America's governance failures is the growing problem of urban crime. Though crime in the region has always been a serious issue given Latin America's robust illicit economy, it has acquired a new dimension. From Mexico City to Buenos Aires, citizens have lost the right to walk the streets without fear. The lack of effective policing and judicial systems—court systems, judges, and prosecutors—breeds a culture of lawlessness and violence. Several small and weak states in the Caribbean and the Andean regions are at risk of becoming permanent centers of drug activity, money laundering, and other criminal operations. Adherence to the rule of law and the administration of justice are critical components that bring stability to democratic regimes. Group members noted that only Chile has effective police forces and regulatory mechanisms that have successfully combated crime and lawlessness.

In addition to the increased level of urban crime, weak governments and institutions prevent democratic progress. Participants stated that the dismal economic and social performance in country after country in Latin America is due to the poor implementation of critical economic reforms designed to combat poverty, unemployment, and inequality. The lack of strong government institutions will continue to hinder the growth of democracy in the region.

Corruption in Political Parties Leads to Populism

The working group also addressed the problem of corruption in Latin

America. According to one participant, corruption is the central theme of national life in the region. Half of all the economic activity in Latin America is said to take place in the informal sector. According to the United Nations, drug sales in the region far exceed the $75 billion in agricultural products that Latin America exports every year. Some of this profit is used to buy off politicians and their parties. Politically influential criminal networks delegitimize political parties. The regional disenchantment with political parties has led to the emergence of and sympathy for populist movements. Since the early 1990s, nearly a dozen elected presidents have been forced from office, many by street protests or mob violence. The mindset in many Latin American countries is that civil society is morally superior to political society. Corruption has created a disconnect between political parties and their constituencies. In fact, many electoral movements in the region now shy away from calling themselves political parties.

Populist movements in the region have capitalized on perceptions of corruption by championing the interests of the poor and powerless. They offer easily comprehensible, if incomplete, solutions to poverty, arguing that the poor will derive benefits once the corrupt elites are cut off from the power of the state. The effects of the populist movement are being felt in countries like Venezuela, where Chávez has capitalized on his anticorruption and antiglobalization platform. Morales made a similar case in Bolivia.

Inequality

Participants noted that Latin America is often described as the most unequal region in the world. Interestingly, they also noted that inequality and exclusion are not new phenomena in the region. Latin America has always suffered from extreme poverty and limited upward mobility. So why has inequality become such a political lightning rod in the region today? One member suggested that globalization makes inequality more visible—an effect felt in all regions of the world, including Africa and Southeast Asia.

Inequality in Latin America has two dimensions that are deeply connected. First, policymakers and the public seemingly view the existence of inequality as the source of justification for the excessive level of crime and violence in the region. In other words, inequality is creating a culture of tolerance for lawlessness. Second, many populist policymakers and a growing percentage of the public believe that globalization and the neoliberal economics of the "Washington Consensus," brought to the region during the late 1980s and 1990s, are the core factors behind the dire inequality, poverty, and exclusivity in the region.

On the other hand, ironically, participants pointed out that though many in the region blame globalization for "savage capitalism," Latin America is perhaps the least globalized and liberalized region in the world. Despite the fact that economic reforms based on the Washington Consensus were initiated in Latin America during the early 1990s, such reforms were never properly or fully implemented. The only country that has reduced poverty, unemployment, and inequality in the region is Chile—the most integrated country in Latin America. Chile has created export markets not only in Latin America and North America but in Asia as well.

Weak States

After September 11, 2001, the U.S. policy community is fully aware of the threats posed by weak states. However, participants noted that weak states in Latin America pose an additional risk to the United States due to the impact of illegal immigrants' use of illicit channels to send their remittances back home. Latin Americans living in the United States send home almost $46 billion annually to their native countries. Though a large portion of this money comes from legal immigrants and flows through legitimate channels, a sizable percentage comes from illegal immigrants who find alternative means to send money home. This procedure helps to fuel transnational crime organizations operating in the region, which brings further instability and corruption to Latin America (and the United States).

The region's porous borders also contribute to the ongoing problem of drug trafficking and gang violence. For many Latin American countries, drugs serve as the primary and most lucrative export. Colombia continues to battle a narcotic-fueled insurgency, while Bolivia is embattled over coca-eradication policies.

Anti-Americanism

Participants concluded that anti-Americanism is on the rise in Latin America. They agreed that this phenomenon is not solely a characteristic of leftist regimes; in Chile, for example, anti-American rhetoric is flowing from leaders on the right. Many Latin Americans are skeptical of Washington's commitment to the region. Several group members concluded that after September 11, 2001, Latin America went from being Washington's "backyard" to being an afterthought of U.S. policymakers. The gap between the rhetoric coming from the United States and the U.S.' actual commitment to the region is striking. Washington's preoccupation with the Iraq war has only aggravated its relationship with Latin America.

Regional resentment directed toward the United States is also fueled by nationalistic leaders in the region, in particular Chávez and Castro. Both leaders use virulent attacks against Washington as part of their political platforms. Though Castro remains in command of the only communist government left in the region, participants agreed that Chávez and his anti-American rhetoric are the greatest political challenge facing the United States from the region.

Even though most participants did agree that anti-Americanism is on the rise in the region, several members noted that in countries where the United States has taken an active policy role, U.S. support is relatively high. Similarly, these participants pointed to the increased numbers of Latin American immigrants entering the United States as evidence of an existing level of support for the U.S.' version of economic opportunity and choice.

Hugo Chávez

More than any other country in Latin America, Venezuela has deteriorated in terms of institutional incapacity, corruption, inequality, and employment opportunities during the past two decades. The discredited political system failed to address critical issues, prompting Venezuelans to seek an alternative. Using rhetoric designed to resonate with many sectors of the country that were denied the fruits of market reforms, Chávez was elected president in 1998 and has remained in power for seven years. A charismatic and shrewd political leader, Chávez has consolidated governmental control and amassed power. Unlike Castro, who governs over a bankrupt state, Chávez is blessed with an oil-rich country and, currently, high market prices for oil.

Group members noted that Chávez has accurately zeroed in on widely felt fundamental grievances in the region—dismal employment generation; acute crises in the provision of healthcare, education, and pension benefits; and inequality. Nevertheless, participants believe that his prescription for these problems would take the region back several decades, when authoritarianism, autocracy, and dictatorships prevailed. With his immense oil wealth, Chávez is funding counter-consensus movements in Bolivia, Ecuador, Peru, and Nicaragua. He has also entered into a variety of agreements with Castro's Cuba, becoming the economic lifeline to the island's failed economy. But there are clear limits to the reach of his appeal, in the view of some participants. It was agreed that the United States should be taking the initiative from Chávez rather than letting him set the regional agenda.

III. STRATEGIC SURPRISES

Given all these factors facing Latin America today, the working group participants posited several strategic surprises that could confront the United States and the Bush administration in the near future. Ultimately, the group identified six possible surprises.

Negative Surprises

- Chávez's populist/counterconsensus movement could spread further in the region;

- Chávez could alter U.S. opportunities to press for change in a post-Castro Cuba;

- A collapse of Chávez's regime could cause the demise of a once rich nation with a powerful democratic tradition—leaving the region with a huge governability problem; and

- Congressional forces could alter U.S. immigration policies, thereby closing a critical exit option that currently exists for the poor in Latin America. The strain caused by such an action could resonate throughout the region and exacerbate all of the factors discussed above.

Positive Surprises

- Uribe's success in Colombia in stabilizing political institutions while combating a drug-financed insurgency could influence other struggling Andean nations; and

- [There are no true surprises in Latin America.] The pro-democracy and pro-market economy orientation of most Latin American countries—despite the trends and concerns identified above—could be sustained and even strengthened with time.

The Spread of Chávez's Populism and a New Ideology

By and large, working group members believed that Chávez is the most potent threat facing the United States in the region, though governance failure generally ranks high as well. Chávez's ability to export his ideas to neighboring nations in the region threatens the stability of already weak and struggling democracies in Nicaragua, Bolivia, Peru, and Ecuador. In Latin America, the inexpensive cost of financing social movements is working in Chávez's favor. As leaders like Morales come to power, democracy in Latin American could suffer a critical setback. Morales' subsequent victory in the Bolivian presidential election affirmed this danger.

Furthermore, Chávez's ambitions are not limited to the Andean region. Several participants noted that he has made clear his intent to forge a wide anti-U.S. coalition in order to replace Washington's agenda for the hemisphere with his own platform rejecting representative constitutional democracy and market economics. Chávez has reached several financial and energy agreements with Argentine President Néstor Kirchner, sealing what Chávez has taken to calling "a Caracas-Buenos Aires axis."

Chávez and Cuba

An interesting dynamic of Chávez's threat is his budding relationship with Castro. Working closely with Cuban intelligence, Chávez has financed the revitalization of a wide range of programs that had grown dormant because Castro lacked the capital to finance them. Before the emergence of Chávez, Castro was effectively isolated in the hemisphere. Given this isolation, Washington assumed that upon Castro's death Cuban communism would come to an end, and the United States would help bring a democratic transition to the island nation. But Castro is not prepared to cede the field and has seen in Chávez not only a rich infusion of petroleum and cash to Cuba at a vital moment but also a way to extend communism once he dies or is incapacitated. One group member noted that Venezuela is now supplying more economic resources to Cuba than the Soviet Union did during the Cold War.

If Chávez continues to bolster Castro's regime in Cuba, the U.S.' ability to shape the transition to democracy in Cuba will be weakened. It is in Washington's best interest to ensure that, upon Castro's death, a Cuban political evolution joins the democratic mainstream and that political chaos and turmoil are kept to a minimum to avoid a costly intervention. The consequences of a U.S. intervention in Cuba would be dramatic (especially given how Latin America responded to the Iraqi intervention).

Chávez's Collapse

Another possible surprise scenario discussed during the meeting was the negative ripple effects that the collapse of Chávez's regime could have on the region. As Chávez continues to consolidate power in what was once a modern democratic state, his ability to govern will grow more difficult. A participant noted that this is indicated already in his use of Cuban intelligence and security services for his protection. He is also relying on the Cubans to help manage social programs in Venezuela. If Chávez's regime does collapse, Venezuela will be left a shell of its former self, giving the hemisphere a huge governability problem to be dealt with.

The Surprise Has Occurred

One participant argued that the real strategic surprise has already occurred in the form of Chávez's consolidation of power and his ability to use oil wealth to play a flamboyant antiestablishment leadership role. He is increasingly a magnet for forces opposing free markets, economic integration, and U.S.-inspired security and counterdrug policies. According to this participant, in 1995 no one would have been able to predict that Venezuela would be aligned with Cuba, leading an anti-American populist movement in the Central American and the Andean region. The United States is witnessing how this is affecting the region, and it should reshape its policies to reflect the change in the political environment in Latin America.

U.S. Immigration Policies

Given Latin America's proximity to the United States, immigration, both legal and illegal, is the root of many frustrations for congressional policymakers. After September 11, 2001, the United States embarked on a program to strengthen border controls and limit the number of immigrants admitted. Immigration reform has several elements, in addition to border control: workplace inspections, visa quotas, guest worker programs, and tracking and removing undocumented residents living in the United States. Unfortunately, many domestic policymakers do not take into account the impact that these

U.S. laws and programs have on countries in Latin America. With all the problems that plague the poor in the region, a major escape valve has always been the possibility of immigrating to the United States. Some participants believed that if the U.S. Congress passes legislation that effectively closes this option to Latin America's poor, frustrations in the region could erupt and have severe repercussions for struggling democracies in the hemisphere.

Uribe's Success

Despite certain negative strategic surprises, participants were also able to point to positive developments in the region for the United States. Under the leadership of President Uribe and the strong support of the United States, the Colombian government has had some success in stabilizing political institutions and combating narcotics-funded insurgencies like the FARC (Fuerzas Armadas revolucionarias de Colombix, or the Revolutionary Armed Forces of Colombia) and the ELN (Ejército de Liberación National, or National Liberation Army). With his recent victory in the Colombian Supreme Court, Uribe won the right to run for a second term—his platform will continue to press for the disarmament of the insurgent groups, in the context of a government-led negotiation strategy, and the advancement of institutional stability. If Colombia continues to make progress in securing its democracy, it could serve as an example to other struggling countries in the Andean region.

However, group members made it clear that challenges still remain for Uribe. Corruption plagues many of Colombia's government institutions, and the FARC still controls vast amounts of land and profits tremendously from the illicit sale of cocaine. Also, human rights groups have complained that Colombia's law and procedures for disarming the paramilitary groups (AUC, or Autodefensas Unidas de Colombia—United Self-Defense Forces of Colombia) fail to punish adequately the perpetrators of past atrocities.

No Surprise at All

A number of comments and exchanges pointed toward the ironic conclusion that perhaps the greatest positive surprise in Latin America is the uncertain and still indeterminate trajectory of regional trends. Though there are plenty of valid concerns and troubling patterns in the region, democratic and market economy principles retain a dominant place and can be bolstered through a range of actions and policies. For this very reason, one wonders if Washington will in fact invest the necessary resources and political capital to "take Chávez's constituency away from him" and reengage effectively in the region. If it does, that would, indeed, be a positive surprise.

IV. POLICY IMPLICATIONS OF POTENTIAL LATIN AMERICAN SURPRISES

In reviewing the strategic surprises and possible scenarios, group members noted the policy options available to the United States to help mitigate and avert further negative surprises while, at the same time, advance positive developments in countries like Colombia and Chile. The options listed included benign neglect, direct confrontation, and indirect confrontation through increased aid and expanded attention dedicated to engaging Latin America. Furthermore, participants suggested a reexamination of domestic immigration policies.

Group members generally agreed that after September 11, 2001, Latin America no longer occupied a central position in U.S. foreign policy. The region lacked the type of critical threats from terrorist organizations, Islamic fundamentalists, and weapons of mass destruction present in the Middle East and Afghanistan. Despite the lack of these types of threats, the working group's discussion suggested that conditions in Latin America require more attention than Washington has been able or willing to offer. Against this backdrop, there was virtually no support within the group for engaging in a policy of benign neglect. Instead, participants believed the U.S. policymakers needed to do a better job of thinking through how to balance diverse policy goals and of consulting more systematically and at higher levels with other key governments in the region.

Regarding Chávez, several group members suggested that the United States directly confront his political platform and isolate him in the region. These participants believed that the United States has enough information to expose Chávez and his corrupt practices. In addition to revealing Chávez's corruption, they also believed the United States should "steal" his constituency. One participant noted that no other country in the world has more to say about successfully opening up political and economic structures to ordinary people and creating upward mobility than the United States. Instead of ignoring the inequality, government incapacity, and corruption faced by many

Latin American countries, U.S. policymakers should speak to these problems, making it clear that there are legitimate democratic and economic ways to solve them.

Many participants were intrigued by the concept of "stealing" Chávez's constituency, but there was some discussion about the method and process of doing so. Some group members believed that such efforts must be conducted through indirect channels like the Organization of American States (OAS), the Inter-American Development Bank, non-governmental organizations (NGOs) like the National Democratic Institute, and regional neighbors to avoid further agitating the anti-Americanism present in the region. Other members believed that the only ones capable of "stealing" Chávez's constituency are the Venezuelans themselves. These members believed that the United States should use the intelligence it has to reveal to the Venezuelans that Chávez is a corrupt official masking his crimes with social rhetoric. Once Chávez is exposed and isolated, his ability to spread his counterconsensus rhetoric will be limited.

On the other hand, many members believed that the United States must not exaggerate the challenge posed by Chávez and other leftist governments in the region. Washington's overly reactive strategic approach in dealing with Chávez in recent years has resulted in major and costly blunders, such as the U.S.' initial support of the unsuccessful April 2002 coup against him. They believed that Washington should mimic its skillful and pragmatic dealings with leaders like Lula in Brazil and Kirchner in Argentina and with other populist regimes in the region.

In terms of developing stronger democratic institutions in Latin America, group members agreed that more funding is required for anticorruption initiatives and programs building government capacity. Emphasis was placed on the critical role that regional neighbors have in helping challenged neighbors. Several participants also noted the vital importance of NGOs in this process. Latin America-focused NGOs need to redirect some of their efforts from democracy promotion and invest more attention to enhancing economic performance. NGOs need to educate elected officials so that they understand the economic issues facing their countries and appreciate the ways in which globalization can advance their economies and ease inequality.

To combat anti-Americanism in the region, several participants suggested increased engagement in countries where this sentiment is most powerful. These participants noted that where U.S. support is historically weakest, Washington has not had a sustained engagement—largely in the Southern Cone region. U.S. support remains high in countries where the United States is fully engaged—Colombia, Mexico, and most countries in Central America. This suggests that with more outreach and greater effort to assert itself, the United States could become a more substantive partner to countries where anti-Americanism predominates.

Finally, sound U.S. immigration policy is critically important to Latin America. Since September 11, 2001, the U.S. Congress has been highly concerned with the problems of illegal immigration. However, some participants believed that immigration to the United States is simply a reaction to the lack of opportunities available to the poor in Latin America. Furthermore, they argued that the benefits of the ongoing wave of immigrants in many cases outweigh the consequences. But, as participants noted, domestic policymakers have reason for concern. The spread of gang violence across borders and drug trafficking propels Congress to push for a more limited immigration policy. Foreign policy strategists and domestic policymakers are faced with a problem with competing interests, and both should consult and work with each other to develop consistent immigration laws and programs.

V. CONCLUSION

Perspectives differed about the precise policy prescription the United States should employ to help mitigate or avoid Latin America's possible surprise scenarios, but there was a consensus that Washington needs to enhance its efforts in the region. Latin America will not easily revert to authoritarianism, even in hard times. But, on the other hand, building consolidated democracies amid weak institutions, inadequate policy implementation, inequality, corruption, and the constant rhetoric from antiestablishment figures like Chávez is a long and arduous job that requires tactful commitment from the United States.

2

Africa: Is Democracy Taking Root?

OVERVIEW

In February 2006, the Schlesinger Working Group continued its series of discussions focusing on democracy in Latin America, Africa, and Southeast Asia. The second meeting, which took place on February 13, discussed "Africa: Is Democracy Taking Root?" After the collapse of the Berlin Wall in 1989, a third wave of democracy swept through the African continent. Statistics show that while Freedom House designated only two African countries as "free" in 1972, by 2005, eleven countries achieved "free" status and nineteen others received a "partly free" designation.[3] Moreover, more than two-thirds of African nations have undergone elections, and the recently established African Union (AU) has decreed that it will not recognize governments that come to power through unconstitutional means. Of Africa's fifty-three countries, thirty of them are now entrenched in what analysts describe as the "consolidation state" of their democratic development. Much of this success can be attributed to the growth and development of civil society organizations, free media, and Africans' continued desire and demand for democratic governance.

Despite this uncontested surge of democratic activity in the early to mid-1990s, some skeptics caution that the trend toward

---

3. eds. Aili, Pino and Arch Puddington. *Freedom in the World 2005: The Annual Survey of Political Rights and Civil Liberties* (Lanham, MD: Rowman & Littlefield Publishers, 2005).

democratic consolidation in Africa stalled after 2002. They point to various factors that plague the region: continentwide institutional incapacity; corruption; lack of decentralization; continuous and renewed conflicts in Sudan, Chad, Uganda, Ethiopia,and Eritrea; fragile civil societies; and inadequate resource management both in terms of economic and human capital. The purpose of the February 13 meeting was to get an overview of these current regional trends to assess whether democracy is progressing in Africa. As part of this effort, the group also explored what strategic surprises may occur for the United States as a result of Africa's struggle toward democratic consolidation. As in the past, the group proposed several policy recommendations to mitigate, avoid, or exploit these possible strategic surprises.

I. SUMMARY

After the discussion, group members agreed that Africa is at a critical juncture, vacillating between continentwide democratic consolidation and political stagnation. A handful of participants pointed to genuine transformations, including the end of apartheid in South Africa and the quelling of civil strife in Mozambique and Sierra Leone, as examples of regional democratic success stories. These group members were also encouraged by the work and commitment of democracy promotion groups and other civil society NGOs such as the Transition Monitoring Group in Nigeria, the Campaign for Democracy and Development in Ghana and Nigeria, and the Campaign for Good Governance in Sierra Leone.

Even so, the majority of group members agreed that since 2002, the spread and development of democracy on the continent has stalled. Given Zimbabwean President Robert Mugabe's ranting against opposition leaders and human rights activists; coup-makers in Togo and the Central African Republic who remain unpunished by the AU and ECOWAS (the Economic Community of West African States); and poorly conducted and contested elections in Guinea (Conakry) and Cameroon, participants wondered whether standards for democratic governance are being whittled down to suit incumbent rulers. Participants also believed that the problem is exacerbated in some cases by a lack of political will on the part of the ruling elite to press for democratic reform and consolidation.

The predominance of these and similar setbacks caused group members to focus on the question of why democracy risks stalling in Africa. After pondering this question, they were able to identify several possible factors and forces that might be impairing continent-wide democratic consolidation. Though these factors are not strategic surprises in and of themselves, they are crucial to understanding Africa's democratic development. Factors and forces mentioned by participants include the following:

- Widespread state incapacity, especially in terms of elections and domestic accountability institutions such as legislatures, courts, civil society, and the media. Institutional incapacity also leads to the inadequate distribution of public goods and services to the general population.

- Lack of loyal and consistent opposition parties, which are a critical vehicle for assuring government accountability.

- Inadequate decentralization of power and authority, which leads to the continuation of ethnic and regional strife, marginalization, and extensive levels of corruption.

- Problems of leadership—some African leaders lack the qualities or motivation for establishing fledgling democratic institutions.

- Challenges of resource management both in terms of human and economic resources, underminng Africa's ability to attain both economic and political development.

- Conflicts in Sudan and Uganda, a troubled transition from war to peace in the Democratic Republic of the Congo (DRC), the threat of renewed violence on the boundary between Ethiopia and Eritrea, and limited security sector reforms, hindering continentwide democratic consolidation.

- The negative effects on a large portion of West Africa from the reverberations of Nigeria's contentious political scene. This problem will also impact the world energy markets as conflict in the Niger Delta continues.

II. FACTORS AND FORCES STALLING AFRICAN DEMOCRATIC CONSOLIDATION

State and Institutional Incapacity

The Group recognized the success of Botswana, Mauritius, Mozambique, and South Africa in implementing and managing regulatory frameworks and oversight mechanisms, as well as the development of regional good governance initiatives such as the African Peer Review Mechanism, which monitors whether participating states' policies and practices accord with agreed political and economic governance norms and standards. However, some participants argued that African democratic development is hindered by electoral malfeasance, weak legislative bodies, desolate judicial systems, fragile civil societies, and poorly funded free media.

A group member noted that free and fair elections are vital to the legitimacy of a democratic government. However, credible elections in Africa are more than matched by the actions of autocratic leaders in countries like Cameroon, Chad, Gabon, Congo, Equatorial Guinea, Togo, Mauritania, and Zimbabwe. Though these leaders conduct elections and spout democratic rhetoric, the elections are marred by purged voter rolls, political patronage, and/or stuffed ballot boxes. These practices diminish popular confidence in the meaning and merits of democratic governance. Nigeria serves as another example of flawed electoral practices. Both its previous two national elections in 1999 and 2004 were blemished by serious voting irregularities, and several participants forecast that Nigeria will again experience rigged elections in 2007.

Participants also stated the importance of domestic accountability institutions in providing a system of checks and balances against an excessively powerful executive/autocrat. Though there are examples of African legislatures and judiciaries blocking third-term aspirations for leaders in Zambia and Malawi, most group members agreed that such events are eclipsed by the prevalence of impotent parliaments and corrupt courts. Togo epitomizes this tendency. After the death of Togolese President Gnassingbe Eyadema, the military banned the speaker of the National Assembly and coerced the remaining members of the National Assembly and the Constitutional Court into validating the coup making Eyadema's son president. Furthermore, most members of African legislatures lack training, resources, and the support of competent and professional staff. In Ethiopia, for example, less than a quarter of parliamentarians have a high school education or a university degree.

Civil society organizations and free media are vital to advancing continentwide democratic governance. Participants agreed that both these institutions represent areas of hope for Africa; civil society is flourishing as never before, while media groups are increasingly vibrant. Nevertheless, at times African civil society groups lack the skills and the political support from elites required to have a lasting influence. They are also subject to the interests of their international backers—these interests do not always parallel democratic development. Likewise, the media suffers from poor funding and a susceptibility to bribery and intimidation.

Finally, the inefficiency and ineffectiveness of state institutions in Africa have left many Africans questioning whether there is a democratic dividend. Many Africans believed that the transition to democracy in the 1990s would lead to an improved distribution of public goods and services to better their standard of living. Ten years later, for the most part these aspirations remain unmet. When democratic government structures fail to deliver, the legitimacy of these institutions is questioned, opening the door for competing political ideologies or pure populist demagoguery. Working group members identified this trend occurring in Latin America with Chávez's Venezuela and Morales' Bolivia. One participant suggested that Africa may start to experience a similar trend stemming from Mugabe's Zimbabwe and Yoweri Museveni's Uganda. However, other members pointed to the Afro Barometer,[4] which indicates that the African public continues to robustly support and demand democratic governance despite the diminishing supply of it.

Absence of a Loyal and Consistent Opposition

Group members were also concerned with many African countries lack of a loyal and consistent opposition. One participant pointed to Senegal, where, after the recent election, the opposition parties switched platforms to join the prevailing party. In Swaziland, opposi-

---

4. The Afro Barometer is an independent, non-partisan research project that measures the social, political, and economic atmospher in Africa, http://www.afrobarometer.org.

tion parties are illegal, while in Zimbabwe they are highly restricted. Without the presence of a loyal and consistent opposition, power rotation, a critical accountability component of democratic governance, is limited. Similarly, group members noted the absence of political party platforms. Without competing platforms highlighting development plans and alternative policy stands, elections are transformed into popularity contests based on the personality and charisma of party leaders, or worse, into ethnic plebiscites.

Participants also pointed to the problem that even where multi-party elections occur, a single party typically dominates. Such was the case in Tanzania and Mozambique's elections in 2004. Even South Africa, considered one of the continent's strongest democracies, is dominated by one political party, the African National Congress.

Inadequate Decentralization of Power

In addition to the issues of government incapacity and weak political opposition, the working group also addressed the problem of centralized power in the executive branch. Political power in a large proportion of African states remains in the hands of one man. For instance, in Cameroon, the president appoints all office holders in the executive branch. In addition, the president has complete control of the judicial branch, because he appoints everyone that holds a position, from Supreme Court judges to local sheriffs. The legislative branch is also rendered powerless, because the constitution of Cameroon authorizes the president to appoint 30 percent of its members to a Senate that has yet to be instituted ten years after the amendment was enacted in 1996. Inadequate decentralization of power and authority often leads to internal tension, as groups are marginalized and deprived of their share of public goods and services. In Nigeria, the overly centralized nature of President Olusegun Obasanjo's government has increased already ripe tensions within the country.

Such centralized distribution of power also leads to excessive corruption. According to Transparency International's *2005 Corruption Perceptions Index,*[5] nineteen African nations were listed among the thirty most corrupt countries in the world, with Chad, Nigeria,

---

5. *2005 Corruption Perceptions Index*, Transparency International (Federal Republic of Germany), http://www.transparency.org/policy_and_-research/surveys_indices/cpi/2005.

Equatorial Guinea, and Côte d'Ivoire listed in the bottom ten. However, group members did point out that efforts by regional and subregional African institutions, as well as by some African governments, are underway to reverse the negative corruption trend. For example, the governments of Nigeria, Lesotho, and Zambia have established successful anticorruption initiatives. Lesotho has indicted several former government officials, and in Zambia, President Levy Mwanawasa's anti-corruption crusade has reached the heart of his own government, with indictments issued to both his vice president and his finance minister.

The Role of Leadership

One group member mentioned the issue of leadership and human agency. Responsible democratic leadership is paramount to the institutionalization of democracy. Here members directed their attention to Seymour Martin Lipset's article, "George Washington and the Founding of Democracy."[6] According to Lipset, by voluntarily retiring from office, George Washington set a precedent exemplifying a proper republican approach to the problem of succession. With some notable exceptions such as Nelson Mandela of South Africa, Sir Seretse Khama of Botswana, Joaquim Chissano of Mozambique, Abdou Diouf of Senegal, and Benjamin Mkapa of Tanzania, many African leaders have been less successful in creating the institutions that are indispensable for carrying on the life of a democratic political society. Instead, Africa's autocrats, democratic rhetoric notwithstanding, retain power and create a sense of disenchantment with democratic governance. For example, Zimbabwe, Gabon, Burkina Faso, Equatorial Guinea, Cameroon, Uganda, Libya, Egypt, and Angola are ruled by presidents who have been in power for twenty years or more.

Many participants see these autocracies as representing a major negative trend; others pointed out a third type of government structure present on the continent. This third group consists of governments struggling through civil wars and coups to get onto the path of democracy. Countries like Liberia, Côte d'Ivoire, Rwanda, Burundi, Sierra Leone, and the DRC can neither be defined as true democracies

---

6. Seymour Martin Lipset, "George Washington and the Founding of Democracy," *Journal of Democracy* 9.4 (1998).

nor can they be grouped with the autocratic regimes listed above. Group members concurred that it is in this middle group of struggling nations that democratic leadership will be essential to building sound institutions where democracy can prosper.

Poor Resource Management

Resource management, both in terms of human and economic capital, is crucial to successful democratic consolidation. Participants agreed that Africa has a long history of inadequate resource management. In terms of human capital, the continent suffers from pandemics, including HIV/AIDS, malaria, tuberculosis, and other diseases that have drained the continent of its workforce. As life expectancy rates drop and social support networks collapse under the weight of high death rates, the struggle for daily survival in African countries risks superseding debate about democratic governance.

Making matters worse, Africa's best and brightest often flee the continent, taking their much-needed skills and experience to Europe or the United States in search of better lives. Several group members believed that the African "brain drain" is depriving the continent of professionals who possess the leadership and management skills that are required to build sound democratic institutions. Various estimates suggest that between 20 and 50 percent of the top African professionals and skilled personnel now reside outside the continent, and most maintain minimal professional contact with the motherland.

While participants agreed that the "brain drain" phenomenon has intensified over the years to the detriment of many African countries, they pointed to efforts of organizations like the AU and the New Partnership for Africa's Development (NEPAD), which are taking steps to reverse this pattern. NEPAD has identified investing in human resource development and reversing the "brain drain" as two of the priority areas for African development. Efforts are ongoing to develop a continentwide human resource development strategy and, under the leadership of the AU, to establish a human resource databank on the African diaspora.

In terms of economic resources, group members noted that Africa is not a poor continent given its natural resources and mineral wealth; rather, participants agreed that Africa, like other places, suffers from the "resource curse." In one example, the much-discussed Chad-Cameroon pipeline project has run into difficulties after the Chad government departed from its commitments to the World Bank, oil companies, and NGOs by insisting on using a greater share of the revenues to purchase arms. Chad's experience highlights a disturbing, yet familiar, challenge: the need for a stable and sustained government commitment to use public funds from newly tapped riches on their people.

Despite these examples, other members pointed to successful efforts toward economic resource management in countries such as South Africa and Mozambique. South African Finance Minister Trevor Manual has successfully reduced the country's budget deficit and implemented infrastructure programs designed to increase South Africa's global competitiveness. Similarly, Mozambique's Prime Minister Luisa Diogo has initiated macroeconomic reform programs to encourage more development and investment. NEPAD has also identified a continentwide agenda for sound economic policies.

Conflict and Security Sector Reform:

Group members agreed that conflicts in Africa have taken a terrible toll on the population and undermined the stability required for continentwide political and economic development. It is also during conflict situations that the most vicious violations of human rights occur: the Rwandan genocide, the periodic massacres in the DRC, and the violent civil war in Liberia. Though the number of wars in Africa has significantly declined in the last five years, participants noted that the threat of conflict remains. Hot conflicts continue in Somalia, Côte d'Ivoire, Sudan—where the conflict in Darfur is now spilling over into neighboring Chad—and in Nigeria's Delta region. Similarly, countries emerging from conflict, such as Liberia, Sierra Leone, Burundi, and the Central African Republic, remain fragile. Ethiopia and Eritrea are on the verge of a renewed border conflict, which would have serious repercussions for the Horn of Africa. Furthermore, the risk of conflict in regional-cornerstone states like Nigeria and Zimbabwe could result in a failing state scenario. Not only would these collapses have negative reverberating effects for the continent on the whole, but they would also pose international security threats. The U.S. embassy bombings in Kenya and Tanzania in August 1998 proved that terrorist organizations are active on the continent. Weak and failed states provide safe havens for terrorists, and radical Islamist networks such as the Al-Ittihad al-Islami movement will continue to seek ways to expand their influence and activities.

Several group members noted that continued conflict in Africa is partly a result of weak security sector reforms. In terms of security sector reforms, participants pointed to Liberia. After years of conflict and civil war, in December 2005 Liberia elected Ellen Johnson-Sirleaf president. Her election presents a tremendous opportunity to restore peace and development in Liberia. However, unless durable reforms are put in place to prevent various armed factions from interfering in the political process, the possibility for renewed violence remains.

Nigeria: A Country and a Continent, Hanging in the Balance

Of all the concerns facing Africa today, working group members were most concerned about how Nigeria's internal struggles will affect the continent's ability to continue democratic development. Despite its history of military rule, Nigeria has been a supporter of democratic transition across Africa, a role that President Obasanjo has expanded. But Nigeria is facing a situation that is tearing at the delicate threads that hold together its vast ethnic and religious population. In the always volatile Niger delta, fresh violence from militants seeking more local control over oil wealth has slashed oil production and helped send prices skyrocketing. Though President Obasanjo chose not to alter the constitution in order to run for a third term in 2007, there are still substantial fears that his successor may not be able to quell the ethnic and religious frictions that have the potential to drag down a large part of the West African region.

III. STRATEGIC SURPRISES

Given all these factors facing Africa today, working group members posited several strategic surprises that could confront the United States and the Bush administration in the near future. The group identified six possible surprise scenarios.

Negative Surprises

- As Chinese investment displaces western economic interests in Africa, the external influences will shift from countries with an interest in democracy promotion to countries that are indifferent to democracy and human rights. Over the medium term, Africa's current stagnation could become a full-scale retreat from democratic standards and practices.

- If President Obasanjo's successor is unable to continue to implement democratic reforms and quell internal discontent, it could result in the destabilization of Nigeria.

- The collapse of key regional countries such as Zimbabwe, Ethiopia, the DRC, and Sudan would create a huge governability problem over vast territories of land and sizable populations as well as the increased likelihood of internal strife.

- The spread of Islamic fundamentalism, amplifying religious tensions throughout the continent, could result in a new terrorist threat to the West.

Positive Surprises

- Liberia's successful transition to a democratic state under the leadership of President Ellen Johnson-Sirleaf could exert a positive influence on other struggling West African nations.

The China Effect

Several participants were concerned with the governance implications resulting from the increased level of investment and trade links between Africa and China. All across the continent, China is acquiring control of natural resource assets, outbidding western contractors on major infrastructure projects, and providing soft loans and other incentives to bolster its competitive advantage. Most disturbing to democracy promotion is China's willingness to use its seat on the UN Security Council to protect some of Africa's most egregious regimes, including Sudan and Zimbabwe, from international sanctions. Moreover, Ethiopia, criticized because of recent election irregularities and its continuing border dispute with Eritrea, called China "its most reliable [trading] partner" and indicated interest in closer military cooperation. Similarly, under pressure from western donors because of corruption in his administration, the president of Kenya, Mwai Kibaki, led a high-level delegation to China to seek aid.

China's increasing demand for resources in Africa is providing an alternative source of support for regimes that chafe under western pressure for democratic reform. China is affecting the patterns of western influence: negative pressures—such as withholding aid or placing limitations on investment to improve an African country's human rights or governing practices—produce less leverage if China is prepared to counterbalance that influence. With western aid and investment pressures neutralized, the United States and other democracies will have to decide if their stance is purely rhetorical or if they should explore other ways of advancing African political reform.

Nigeria[7]

By and large, working group members believed that Nigeria represents the most potent challenge to democratic norms in the region. In April 2007, the country will conduct the first electoral transfer of civilian presidential power since independence in 1960. Also at stake during the elections are Nigeria's thirty-six governorships. Though the election date is set, for a country more familiar with military dictatorship than democratic rule there is a long way to go if a free and fair election is to take place.

For a start, the country's electoral commission is wrapped up in red tape, accused by members of the National Assembly of inflating costs and by some politicians of showing bias. The electoral commission has barely started the monumental task of registering the country's voters and is unlikely to be equipped to deal with Nigeria's predilection for serious vote rigging.

Divisions within the ruling People's Democratic Party (PDP) could also undermine the election. The PDP was conceived as a vehicle to bind Nigeria's diverse ethnic and political interests together in support of Obasanjo's presidential candidacy in 1999. It won landslide victories in elections that year and again in 2003. But now the party has split. Analysts argue that Obasanjo appointed too many of his friends to posts in the party bureaucracy when he bid for a third term, and the party is now struggling to find a consensus candidate. The splits in the elite are unnerving, considering the bloody sectarian violence that often accompanies political divisions in Nigeria. The country is divided between Christians and Muslims and split between three main ethnic groups and hundreds of minorities. The debate over Obasanjo's successor is centered on whether his successor

---

7. Some ideas expressed in this section were not discussed during the February 2006 meeting. This section was revised in October 2006.

should come from the Muslim-dominated north or the Christian-dominated south.

Adding to the general air of uncertainty is the rising tension in the oil-producing Delta region. The failure to distribute oil revenue equitably has driven local ethnic-rights movements toward greater violence. According to the International Crisis Group, since January 2006 the Movement for the Emancipation of the Niger Delta and other armed groups have waged an increasingly violent campaign against the federal government and foreign oil companies. Obasanjo has ordered a security crackdown in the Delta, but that will achieve little without a coherent plan for political reconciliation there.

Given the level of uncertainty surrounding Nigeria's upcoming election, some participants questioned whether President Obasanjo's successor will be able to save the country from splintering apart. In this period of great instability, the country may collapse under the heavy burden of internal grievances and the corrosive effects of corruption, destabilizing the huge subregion in which it is the leading actor.

Failed States

Another possible surprise scenario discussed during the meeting was the negative ripple effects that the collapse of key states would have on their respective regions. In addition to Nigeria's possible collapse, participants pointed to Zimbabwe, where President Mugabe, the once vaunted liberation leader, rules with a tyrannical fist. The situation in Zimbabwe, with the collapsing economy, four million people in need of food aid, the migration to neighboring countries of as many as three million Zimbabweans, and the growing internal strife, all points to a potential collapse of the state. Not only would this lead to a huge governability problem in a key southern African state, it would also have a major impact on neighboring nations, which would be burdened with refugees, disruption of regional infrastructure, and political violence spilling across borders.

Ethiopia also risks a possible political breakdown. In spite of an open and democratic campaign, Ethiopia's parliamentary elections held on May 15, 2005, fell far short of international standards because of irregularities and postelectoral violence. Opposition parties staged demonstrations that quickly turned violent. The government reacted by jailing the opposition leaders and charging them with treason. Given the increased levels of violence and the government's heavy-handed reaction, the possibility of resolving the conflict by peaceful means (for example, by forming a coalition government, conducting a new election, or setting an agreement for the opposition to take its seats in the parliament) appears unlikely. Instead, the threat of increased military-backed rule and further instability could result in the collapse of the government, leaving the Horn of Africa with a significant governability dilemma.

Furthermore, more than five years after the Lusaka cease-fire agreement, the transition to democracy in the DRC remains fragile. While President Joseph Kabila has made significant progress in liberalizing domestic political activity, establishing a transitional government, and undertaking economic reforms in cooperation with the World Bank and the International Monetary Fund, serious human rights problems remain in the security services and justice system. Moreover, though the first general elections since independence from Belgium in 1960 were held in July 2006, there is fear that the upcoming presidential runoff election might be delayed or experience irregularities. If this delicate election process fails, the country risks tumbling back into a conflict, ensnaring regional neighbors such as Rwanda, Uganda, Burundi, Angola, and Namibia.

Similarly, Sudan also faces serious challenges that could lead to the collapse of the government. Given the country's diverse ethnic populations—majority Muslim, but with a strong minority of Christians in the south—participants agreed that Sudan remains a political powder keg. After emerging from roughly twenty years of civil war between the north and the south, the warring factions agreed to restructure the government, giving representation to the south and opposition parties in the north. However, such redistribution of power has yet to be secured. Making matters worse, the conflict and human rights abuses in the western Darfur region continue. The conflict in Darfur has killed more than two hundred thousand people and forced two million villagers from their homes. On May 5, 2006, the Sudanese government and the largest of the Darfur rebel groups signed a cease-fire agreement intended to end the conflict. Shortly thereafter, the UN Security Council also voted to send in a peacekeeping force to replace the undermanned AU force. However, the cease-fire agreement has collapsed, and Khartoum has expelled the UN envoy. The likelihood of political breakdown in Sudan increases daily, and the vicious human rights abuses continue without an end in sight.

Islamic Fundamentalism and Terrorism

A few group members cautioned that the rise of Islamic militancy may lead to increased terrorist activities on the continent. These participants pointed to Africa's permeable borders, which allow access to countries where there are large populations of discontented and unemployed Muslims as potential recruits for terrorist networks. One participant stated that there had been credible reports that diverse outside radical Islamists continue to form local partnerships in hopes of attacking western targets in Nigeria and South Africa. Complicating the situation, U.S. vulnerability to terrorism in Africa remains high because most embassies, commercial facilities, and humanitarian organizations are less secure than in other areas of the world.

Liberia's Opportunity

Despite negative strategic surprises, participants were able to point to the recent election in Liberia of Africa's first female president, Ellen Johnson-Sirleaf, as a potential positive surprise. Ms. Johnson-Sirleaf's election is a critical step in Liberia's transition from a violent civil war to a peaceful democratic environment. She inherits a nation afflicted by fourteen years of civil war: The country's public works are in shambles; there is no piped-in-water and no electricity grid; and its roads, schools, and health centers, where they still exist, barely function. Nonetheless, if she succeeds, Liberia could serve as an inspiring example to other struggling West African nations.

Another positive dimension stemming from Ms. Johnson-Sirleaf's election is that through her tactfully skilled campaign rhetoric she has won African women new respect in the political scene. Once dominated by male autocrats, many African countries now have women in high positions, and a handful may elect to follow in Ms. Johnson-Sirleaf's footsteps to the pinnacle of democratic power.

IV. IMPLICATIONS FOR U.S. POLICY

In reviewing the combination of factors and forces delaying African democratic consolidation as well as the various strategic surprises arising from the continent, participants evaluated the policy options available to the United States to help alleviate and avert the negative factors and surprises while, at the same time, to advance positive developments in countries emerging from conflict.

Africa is a region of growing vital importance to U.S. national interests. Group members discussed the tension emerging in U.S. African policy between promoting democracy, ensuring stability, advancing energy security and other economic interests, and fighting terrorism. Given these competing policy interests, some participants believed that U.S. policymakers need to do a better job of thinking through how to balance diverse policy goals and enhance bilateral and multilateral partnerships geared toward African political and economic development while maintaining access to energy resources across the Gulf of Guinea region.

Regarding aid policy, participants agreed that the United States should continue to send direct assistance for democracy promotion efforts—election financing, political party training, and NGO support. However, several participants stated that it is important for the United States to build more partnerships with African democrats so that democratic development is not perceived to be a unilateral assignment of the U.S. government. According to these group members, significantly more aid should be directed toward local democracy-based civil-society organizations, both at the national and the regional levels. Local groups can target their efforts more legitimately and consistently on key issues such as respect for the rule of law, state and institutional capacity building, and non-violent strategies for change. Some group members believed that aid policy should go further to try to identify and reward countries and leaders that are good democratic performers. Others warned that U.S. aid may help sustain the patronage networks present in most African countries—aid can perversely prop up leaders who would otherwise be removed for failing to live up to the social contract with their constituents. Another key factor is Africa's diversity: It would be unrealistic to have one policy that fits the needs of fifty-three diverse countries.

In terms of how to prioritize U.S. aid efforts, several group members discussed a policy focusing on conflict states and states in political transition. However, Congress has slashed democratization funds for Africa, leaving critically important countries like Nigeria, Kenya, Uganda, Liberia, and Zimbabwe with insufficient aid amounts. According to these participants, the United States must reverse this trend and dedicate more resources to these countries in order to display a consistent presence and support for African democratic consolidation.

Many participants also stressed that the quality of individual leadership can be decisive in permitting states to move beyond personalized power to the rule of law and constitutional government. Lack of or disregard for term limits is endemic in many African countries. Several group members argued that the United States needs to take a more proactive stance to foster peaceful political transitions, including not only negative leverage tactics like isolation and coercion but also amnesty and "soft landings." In other words, if democracy is the ultimate goal, instead of seeking to criminalize these leaders, U.S. policymakers should pursue all measures to get them to leave office.

Other members suggested that the United States should increase aid to the AU and other subregional institutions. By developing these African-based institutions, the United States can help create more powerful entities that are able to nurture those who favor democracy and nonviolent approaches in Africa. Strong pro-democracy regional institutions can also impose legitimate pressure on regimes that refuse to step down.

In terms of the "brain drain" phenomenon, several participants were concerned with the U.S. Diversity Visa Program, which is designed to attract skilled Africans to the United States. This program has become the primary vehicle for the increased flow of Africans and their families to the United States. According to statistics from the U.S. Citizen and Immigration Services,[8] the number of African green card lottery winners jumped from 16,310 to 20,337 between 2002 and 2004. As these numbers continue to grow, Africa will lose the very leaders it needs to continue on its path toward democratic consolidation. Though there are clear benefits for the United States in continuing this policy, these participants argued that there are also benefits to working with African countries to encourage economic development, which is the only way to curb the exodus of Africa's professional workforce.

When dealing with China's growing influence in Africa, participants agreed that the United States must not exaggerate the challenge. China is a legitimate competitor for natural resources, and the United States retains many advantages on which to build. Group

---

8. See International Organization for Migration, *World Migration Report 2005* (Geneva: International Organization for Migration, June 2005).

members believed that there is a large reservoir of good will toward the United States in Africa as well as recognition of the importance of the United States to Africa's hopes for a larger role in the global economy. Therefore, the United States should continue to press African leaders on governance, transparency, and human rights issues.

V. SUMMARY CONCLUSION

Democracy promotion cannot be the sole policy prescription for the United States in Africa, given the multiplicity of issues facing the region, the array of likely negative surprise scenarios, and the diversity of U.S. interests. Nonetheless, participants concurred with the need for focused policies that enhance continentwide respect for the rule of law, state capacity and institution building, and increased aid to the AU and subregional institutions, so that they can promote democracy and provide adequate shelters for democrats who have the courage to stand up to autocrats. At the same time, group members noted that it is necessary for U.S. policymakers to prioritize efforts toward countries they deem critical to African democratic development.

Given the significant risk that democracy in Africa may be hijacked or thwarted, policymakers face an arduous task that will no doubt require considerably greater levels of commitment from the United States and its democratic allies.

3
Southeast Asia's Democratic Challenge: Strength (and Weakness) in Diversity

OVERVIEW

The Schlesinger Working Group continued its series of discussions focusing on regional democracy trends with a May 23 session on "Southeast Asia's Democratic Challenge: Strength (and Weakness) in Diversity." Southeast Asia has a broad political spectrum, including democracies of more than a decade's standing (Thailand and the Philippines); more recent democratic experiments (Indonesia and East Timor); semiauthoritarian states that permit multiparty contests in which the dominant party invariably wins (Malaysia, Singapore, and Cambodia); one-party systems in which economic liberalization is encouraged but political challenge to the regime is forbidden (Vietnam and Laos); and authoritarian states in which one person or party rules absolutely (Burma and Brunei).

The breadth of political systems in the region results from several factors: religious, racial, and ethnic diversity; significant differences in levels of economic development; diverse colonial masters; and lingering polarization after the Cold War. Such diversity makes it difficult to discern broad political regional trends. Some analysts maintain that politics in the region are quiescent and nondemocratic. Others argue that despite the persistent backsliding and constant outliers like Burma and Brunei, on the whole the region enjoys an unprecedented degree of healthy political contestation compared to its past.

The purpose of the May 23 meeting was to assess the progress of democracy in Southeast Asia and identify potential policy implications. The working group also explored possible scenarios stemming from the region that might be in store for the United States.

I. SUMMARY

Though group members agreed that the region has a broad political spectrum, they disagreed on the status of Southeast Asia's democratic transition. Several participants cautiously contended that Indonesia's successful democratization, combined with ongoing democratic consolidation efforts in Thailand and the Philippines, might be the beginning of a broad democratic trend in the region. Optimistic members also pointed out that Indonesia's political climate continues to do well as a result of the market reform efforts of President Susilo Bambang Yudhoyono. Despite the string of traumas, from Suharto to the tsunami, the government of Indonesia is moving out of crisis mode and toward a bright democratic future. Some group members also argued that although Southeast Asia has not been immune to the global rise of political Islam, particularly in recent years, Indonesia and Malaysia's practice of political inclusion has helped to keep Islam in the region on the moderate side. To date, it has marginalized the most radical parties in Indonesia (which historically only draw 2–3 percent of the vote) and has led PAS (Parti Islam SeMalaysia, or Islamic Party of Malaysia), the fundamentalist opposition party in Malaysia, to forswear violence in order to remain politically viable.

Some participants questioned the indiscriminate use of the term "democracy" in the region. These members argued that though several countries have democratic institutions, such institutions operate in a fairly authoritarian manner. Examples include countries like Singapore, Cambodia, Malaysia, and Vietnam. These countries are also examples where periods of stability and economic growth have anchored the current regimes, making democratic reform unlikely in the near future. Several group members were also troubled by the internal coup in the Burmese military junta that pushed out quasi-reformer Khin Nyunt and elevated hard-liner Than Shwe, thereby diminishing the ability of western policies to encourage democratization in Burma. There was also a considerable level of concern regarding the region's two democratic stalwarts. In Thailand, a protracted "people's power" movement has forced out the only prime minister to have won an absolute electoral majority. In the Philippines, elite and popular discontent with President Gloria Arroyo since her narrow 2004 electoral victory has essentially delegitimized her administration.

Though participants debated the overall regional democratic trends, they were able to pinpoint a number of formidable challenges that could hinder future democratic development. Some of these challenges affect the region as whole, while others affect specific groups of countries or individual nations. These include the following:

- The regional absence of the "demonstration effect." In other words, the democratization (or slide into authoritarianism) of one country will not necessarily affect the political development of another, which limits the influence and leverage of regional actors like the Association of Southeast Asian Nations (ASEAN).

- The personalized nature of politics in the region. This inhibits political party development. Instead of being organized around platforms and agendas, several of the region's political parties serve as their leader's personal entourage. Such systems also encourage high levels of corruption.

- The hollowness of democratic institutions. This impairs the distribution of public goods and services and reduces the effectiveness of critical reforms. It also limits upward mobility outside of the military; encourages competing political ideologies; and, in some countries, results in population decline as citizens search for better opportunities abroad.

- The powerful interlocking grids among the incumbent party, select business firms, and the military. These allow the groups to gain tight control over the political economy, which leads to limited democratic regime change and the perpetuation of the military's involvement in politics in the region.

- The insufficient decentralization of power. This leads to provincial frustration and violence. Or, where performance decentralization is occurring, performance challenges are created as local governments are suddenly responsible for delivering all basic government services.

- Burma's gridlocked political situation. This continues to challenge ASEAN, the one regional entity that has the potential to press for regional democratic reform.

II. CHALLENGES FACING SOUTHEAST ASIA

The Absence of the Demonstration Effect

Due to the region's political diversity, there is often less demonstration effect in Southeast Asia's democratization than in regions such as Latin America or Africa. As a result, states have limited leverage to influence the political course of their neighbors—a fact that participants noted continues to hinder ASEAN's attempts to promote reconciliation between the military regime and the National League for Democracy in Burma. Though ASEAN was successful in influencing Burma to step aside and not take the association's chair position in 2006, it is losing effectiveness and interest in pressing for Burmese political reform.

Group members were also concerned with the absence of the demonstration effect and how that absence would dilute the positive ripple effects of Indonesia's successful democratic transition from reaching regional neighbors like Malaysia. Malaysia's newly minted Prime Minister Abdullah Badawi received good marks for his economic policy and his liberalizing tendency with regard to the media, civil society, and the range of public policy topics that are now permissible to discuss. Despite these advances, few participants believed there was any likelihood of Badawi pressing for democratic reforms.

On the other hand, participants pointed out that the absence of the demonstration effect in Southeast Asia is not entirely negative. Though it does limit the leverage of democratic regimes in the regime, it equally impairs authoritarian regimes from influencing their neighbors.

The Personalization of Political Parties

Thailand, the Philippines, and Indonesia all have extremely fluid political party systems that are organized around individual personalities. Instead of relying on party platforms and alternative policy stands, elections in these countries are transformed into popularity contests based on the personality and charisma of party leaders. Participants pointed to Thailand's recent political crisis as an example of the negative effects of overly personalized political parties. For example, although Prime Minister Thaksin Shinawatra was forced to step down after his April 2006 election victory, six weeks later he agreed to return to power as the caretaker prime minister. Several participants believed that he took this position to breathe life back into his Thai Rak Thai Party, which was suffering from defections. The situation in the Philippines is more disturbing. In February, President Arroyo declared a national emergency for ten days after rumors of a military coup against her were circulated. The Armed Forces of the Philippines, which former President Ferdinand Marcos had personalized to the point of making it his praetorian guard, is still not fully professionalized. Indonesia's political parties, though still personalized, are developing. And President Yudhoyono's Democratic Party was elected on a platform of economic, anti-corruption, and decentralization reforms.

Participants also discussed the limited political party development in the semi-authoritarian governments in the region. Singapore's ever-ruling People's Action Party (PAP) continues to place limits on opposition parties. Members pointed to the government's tight restrictions on political protest and its repeated use of defamation suits against opposition leaders. Such actions have allowed the PAP to win all ten elections since Singapore's independence. Despite these actions, opposition parties are permitted to take part in elections, which is not the case in Vietnam, Laos, Burma, or Brunei. During Singapore's election in May 2006, opposition parties were allowed to hold large campaign rallies that were moderately covered by the government-friendly local media. Though the opposition successfully put up candidates for more than half of the eighty-four constituency districts, it only won two seats. Critics of the government blame the tight restrictions imposed on opposition parties for the poor results, but Lee Kuan Yew, who was prime minister from 1960 to 1990, defended the government by calling the opposition parties disorganized and stating that "Singapore needs a world-class opposition, not this riffraff."

Political party systems that are organized around individual personalities, or are one-party dominant, often lead to high levels of corruption. According to Transparency International's 2005 *Corruption Perceptions Index*,[9] six Southeast Asian nations ranked poorly on the list of 159 countries. Burma ranked 156; Indonesia ranked 140; Cambodia ranked 131; the Philippines ranked 124; Laos ranked

---

9. *2005 Corruption Perceptions Index*, Transparency International.

77; and Thailand ranked 60. Interestingly, Singapore was the exception, ranking higher than the United States, Great Britain, and Germany.

Hollow Democratic Institutions

The inefficiency and ineffectiveness of state institutions in Southeast Asia impair the distribution of public goods and services and reduce the effectiveness of critical reforms that are necessary for improving social mobility. Several participants pointed to the Philippines, where hollow democratic institutions have helped drive a large percentage of the population to leave the country to find more stable and lucrative work abroad. A member estimated that 10 percent of Filipinos now live and work overseas. Not only does this raise brain drain concerns in specific sectors such as nursing and engineering, but it also deprives the nation of the very individuals it needs to build up effective and stable institutions. Complicating the issue, poorer Filipinos who are unable to seek overseas employment continue to join the military, as it remains the only avenue for social mobility, and it is perceived as the only institution that can change society. Other members argued that weak government institutions also lead to competing political ideologies and populist movements. Participants identified this trend as occurring in Latin America with Chavez's Venezuela and Morales' Bolivia. Although Southeast Asia's populist movements are not as advanced as those found in Latin America, both Thailand and the Philippines have experienced such movements in the past five years.

Though several Southeast Asian countries suffer from impotent state institutions, some group participants were encouraged by Indonesia's impressive efforts to bring efficiency to its government institutions. For the past eighteen months, President Yudhoyono has pushed through critical reforms, including revamping the civil service, rewriting tax laws, raising electricity rates, and imposing civilian control over the maverick armed forces. Yudhoyono is also pursuing more liberal economics to jump-start the Indonesian economy and improve growth rates. By pressing for these difficult reforms, Yudhoyono is constructing stable institutions that should provide avenues of opportunity for future generations of Indonesian citizens.

Interlocking Grids of Power

Another problem that prevents democratic reform and encourages corruption in the region is the presence of interlocking grids among the ruling party, select business firms, and the military. Through corrupt practices and agreements, these groups are capitalizing on political cleavages and using these advantages to benefit economically by maintaining the status quo. As an example of this trend, group members pointed to Malaysia, where the United Malays National Organization (UMNO)—a founding member of the *Barisan Nasional* coalition—has ruled the country uninterruptedly since its independence in 1957. Though Prime Minister Abdullah Badawi has cut costly mega-projects that were initiated by his predecessor, he has predictably shown little enthusiasm for reforms that would break UMNO's dominance. Group members also noted that Cambodia's Prime Minister Hun Sen is trying to convince the opposition party, Sam Rainsy, to join his coalition, which will help continue his rule, dating back to 1979.

Decentralization

Participants were also concerned with the rate of decentralization of power in Southeast Asia. Overly centralized regimes in the region often result in provincial frustration and violence. In some cases, lack of decentralization encourages separatist movements. Separatist groups view the central government as distant and nonresponsive to their needs. For example, in the Philippines, Islamic separatist groups in Mindanao continue to seek independence through acts of violence. Similar movements are present in Thailand's three southern provinces: Pattani, Yala, and Narathiwat. As the largest country in the region, Indonesia also suffers from separatist movements. Recently, the government was able to quell rebel violence and achieve a peace accord in Aceh, but it has not yet been successful in dealing with political dissent and violence in Papua.

Group members noted that Indonesia has initiated dramatic decentralization reforms. Interestingly, the government decided to bypass power transfer to the provincial governments out of fear that it might increase separatist movements. Instead, it transferred authority directly to local district-level governments in hopes of preventing future violence. Unfortunately, since the transfer of power was more immediate than incremental, the reforms have experienced limited success as 450 separate, ill-equipped, and underfunded local government structures continue to struggle to deliver almost all basic government services.

Burma's Instability

Participants agreed that Burma's instability is a serious factor impairing democratic reform not only inside the country but regionally as well. For nearly two decades, international pressure has not been able to produce sustainable gains in political liberalization that could lead to Burmese democratization, and Senior General Than Shwe's rise to power has only aggravated the situation. The regional effects of Burma's instability are most deeply felt in ASEAN. The organization has grown weary of western pressures to force political reforms. Without a regional force providing pressure on the military regime, the likelihood of any democratic political reform in Burma in the near future is doubtful, according to group members.

III. STRATEGIC SURPRISES

Given these challenges facing Southeast Asia, members of the working group identified five surprise scenarios that could confront the United States and the Bush administration in the near future.

Negative Surprises

- The resurgence of rural NPA (the New People's Army—the military-wing of the Communist Party of the Philippines) could lead to the destabilization of one of the region's oldest democracies.

- Separatist movements in Papua and terrorist threats from Jemmah Islamiyah (JI) and other radical jihadist groups in Indonesia could result in a more authoritarian government structure.

- Radical Islamists could gain influence in Malaysia and Indonesia, which would increase the probability of another terrorist attack against western interests.

- Burma could deteriorate into civil war, leaving the region with a major humanitarian crisis and political vacuum.

Positive Surprise

- Indonesia's democratization changes the balance in ASEAN and modifies the group's cardinal principle of noninterference in the affairs of member states, which could lead to a more organized regional effort to pressure authoritarian regimes in the region.

Resurgent NPA in the Philippines

There was measurable anxiety among group members regarding the instability present in the Philippines today. Exacerbating this concern, a resurgent NPA may undermine Philippine democratic institutions, some participants posited, as government power would be consolidated at the highest levels to battle the insurgency. The military wing of the Communist Party of the Philippines, the NPA is a Maoist group formed in March 1969 with the aim of overthrowing the government through protracted guerrilla warfare. In 2003, the United States placed the NPA on its terrorist blacklist, thereby choking off sources of overseas funding for the group. Peace talks with the communists, brokered by Norway, stalled in August 2004 when Manila refused to help persuade the United States and some Western European states to remove the NPA from the terrorism blacklists. Since that time, the NPA has stepped up its violence. It is estimated that there are roughly eight thousand members and the group is active in sixty-nine of the Philippines' sixty-nine provinces. Given President Arroyo's already turbulent tenure in office, a powerful uprising by the NPA would only further impair the government's ability to translate democratic governance into effective governance.

Other members of the group were not convinced that an NPA uprising would ultimately result in the collapse of democracy in the Philippines, citing the strong basic commitment of the people to the practice of democracy. Though the NPA has increased its numbers slightly and is touted as a threat by the Philippine government, these members believe the NPA survives primarily because of its well-entrenched patronage system in the Luzon rural areas, not because there is a new national movement in sympathy with it.

Indonesia's Possible Return to Authoritarianism

Like the Philippines, Indonesia faces domestic separatist groups. Making matters worse, the country also has to deal with terrorist threats from JI and other radical jihadist groups. Though political inclusion has helped to keep Islam in the country on the moderate side, foreign Wahabbi and other radical forces are determined to "purify" the Indonesian Muslims. Several participants were concerned that due to growing threats from these groups, the Indonesian government will revert to a more authoritarian approach to deal with such pressures. Indonesian democracy is nascent, and its citizens have yet to develop the same commitment to democratic government as is present in the Philippines. A setback of this magnitude would not only threaten Indonesian democratic consolidation, but it would also prevent any chance of ASEAN transforming into a regional promoter of good governance and political reform.

Political Islam

In addition to Indonesia's possible return to authoritarianism, a few participants cautioned that the rise of Islamic militancy may also lead to increased terrorist activities in Southeast Asia. Islamic fundamentalists are present in Malaysia, Indonesia, the Philippines, and Thailand, and, as one member noted, Saudi sources continue to funnel financial support to these groups in an effort to incite Wahabbist reform. The region is not immune to terrorist activities. The JI-linked bombings in Bali on October 12, 2002, killed nearly two hundred people (mostly westerners). JI has also been connected to the bombings in Jakarta at the JW Marriott (August 2004) and the Australian embassy (September 2004). Though JI has weakened in strength due to regional and global antiterrorism efforts, many group members believe that its threat still persists.

Burma's Collapse

Participants concurred that Burma represents the greatest challenge to democratic norms in the region. Senior General Than Shwe has shown little concern about the fate of the average Burmese citizen. Much of the population lives without basic sanitation or running water. In 2000, the World Health Organization ranked Burma among the lowest countries worldwide in healthcare delivery to its citizens. High infant mortality rates and short life expectancies further highlight poor health and living conditions. The HIV/AIDS epidemic poses a serious threat to the Burmese population, as do tuberculosis and malaria. There are also numerous documented human rights violations and internal displacement of ethnic minorities. Such conditions have forced several million Burmese to flee to neighboring countries like Bangladesh, India, China, and Thailand to seek work and asylum. More than 160,000 Burmese live in the nine refugee camps in Thailand and the two in Bangladesh, while hundreds of thousands of other Burmese work and reside illegally in the countries in the region.

Given these dismal conditions inside the country, group members voiced concerns regarding the possibility of further internal dissention within the ruling junta that might lead to greater destabilization and ultimately result in a civil war. The devastating consequences of such an event would be a full-blown humanitarian crisis, and, perhaps, a failed state scenario.

ASEAN's Voice for Democratization

A handful of participants were hopeful that Indonesia's democratization might result in a shift in ASEAN's policy of noninterference. Currently, ASEAN operates using a consensus process that favors the least common denominator. In other words, countries like Vietnam and Laos, the tacit leaders of ASEAN's authoritarian states, have the ability to block attempts to give ASEAN a greater role in pressing for regional norms that promote political liberation and human rights protection. With Indonesia's transformation, Southeast Asia's population is demographically democratic, a fact that these group members believe might influence Indonesia and other democracies in the region to dominate ASEAN and advocate for good governance and democratic reforms. If Indonesia were to step up and assume a democratic leadership role in ASEAN, these participants are hopeful that regional pressure would eventually be successful in forcing transition and democratic reforms in Southeast Asia's semiauthoritarian and authoritarian governments.

IV. U.S. POLICY IMPLICATIONS

After discussing the combination of challenges to democracy in Southeast Asia, as well as the possible scenarios that may result, group members evaluated the policy options available to the United States to deal with potential negative surprises and to advance positive developments in the region.

There was wideranging debate over whether democracy promotion should be the major objective of U.S. foreign policy in Southeast Asia. A handful of group members challenged encouraging democracy in Southeast Asia, because the results may in some cases produce unfavorable consequences for U.S. interests. Pointing to the negative results of elections in Palestine, Iran, Bolivia, and Venezuela, these members feared that a U.S. Southeast Asian policy based on democracy promotion would result in a similar series of populist setbacks. On the other hand, some members countered that although convergence of U.S. interests in the short term is not always assured, accountable, law-abiding democratic governments in the region are more likely than authoritarian regimes to promote international peace and combat global terrorism.

Another group of participants argued that instead of supporting democracy for its own sake, the United States should support democratization for instrumental reasons, depending on different political, cultural, and regional contexts. These group members suggested that democracy promotion serves a range of interests in Latin America, Africa, and the Middle East. In Latin America and the Middle East, democracy promotion is critical to preserving the security of the United States and its interests, and it provides a procedural political process to bring accountability and improved governance to African nations. It is possible that Southeast Asia lacks rationales that would dictate a U.S. decision to make democracy promotion a critical component of its regional policy.

Though there was little agreement on whether or not democracy promotion should be a critical component of U.S. foreign policy in the region, there was strong support for policies that promote good governance and the rule of law. Participants favored continued economic support to nongovernmental institutions and regional actors like ASEAN. There was also considerable support for continuation of diplomatic pressure on countries with egregious human rights records. Other policy recommendations included encouraging continued economic development to strengthen Southeast Asia's middle class and providing support to regional and national anticorruption measures and institutional capacity-building programs.

In terms of pressing for Burma's democratization, there was considerable debate over what policy the United States should pursue to positively influence the situation. Due to the U.S.' existing sanctions policies, participants believed there was little the United States could do directly to affect the Burmese government. A few group members were hopeful that the United States could work with regional powers like China, Japan, and India, and regional organizations like ASEAN, to pressure the Burmese military to reform and improve upon its human rights record. Other members believed that this option was unrealistic; both Japan and ASEAN have made previous unsuccessful attempts to rein in the Burmese government and have lost interest. These participants also believed that even if India and China were to engage the Burmese military, there is no assurance that the junta would heed their advice. Several group members argued that it is time that U.S. policymakers change the nature of the debate about Burma from a democratic problem to a humanitarian crisis and enlist the UN Security Council to take action. These participants contend that America's current policy based on economic sanctions is to blame for the U.S.' limited influence on Burma. By shifting the policy debate and terminating sanctions, U.S. policy options will no longer be constrained, and a more nuanced approach might be more productive.

Despite a number of negative developments in the region, participants agreed that the United States needed to step up its efforts to reach out to countries like Indonesia, Thailand, and the Philippines. Group members argued that by becoming a more assertive partner to the region's democracies, the United States may be able to influence ASEAN's transformation to a regional promoter of good governance and human rights.

V. CONCLUSION

Although perspectives differed regarding whether the United States should prioritize policies that promote further democratization in Southeast Asia, group members did agree that the United States should play a more substantive role in the region. Democracy promotion may not be the top objective; however, elements of this policy, like institutional capacity building, anticorruption, political pluralism, and human rights, are all vital in a region where semiauthoritarian and authoritarian nations still persist. To be successful in this effort, participants agreed that the United States must take a more differentiated approach to the region. By doing so, the United States might at least prevent current democracies from reverting back to authoritarian practices and may even assure constructive development in countries like Singapore, Malaysia, Vietnam, Laos, Cambodia, Brunei, and Burma.

ADDENDUM

On September 19, 2006, the Thai military ousted civilian Prime Minister Thaksin in a bloodless coup amid charges of corruption and abuse of power by the former leader. Once heralded as one of Southeast Asia's democratic success stories, Thailand has, at least temporarily, reverted back to authoritarianism. In response, the United States suspended military aid to the country and urged a rapid return to democracy. The regional implications of Thailand's democratic demise may prove to be severe. First, the actions of the Thai junta, combined with the muted international response, may embolden the militaries in other Southeast Asian democracies. For example, in the Philippines, President Arroyo faces renewed rumors of a possible military coup. Second, with Thailand's reversion, Southeast Asia's balance shifts away from constitutional rule—a fact that will inhibit Indonesia and other democracies in the region from leading ASEAN and advocating for good governance and democratic reforms.

Whither Democracy Promotion?

OVERVIEW

After holding meetings on Latin America, Africa, and Southeast Asia, the Schlesinger Working Group concluded its series examining regional democracy trends with a final session on September 6, 2006, focused on U.S. democracy promotion. The session began by looking at the global democratization picture. According to Freedom House's annual survey, the state of freedom throughout the world has continued on an upward trend for the past thirty years.[10] As of 2006, 46 percent of the world's countries were classified as "free," and 30 percent were considered "partially free." Some analysts suggest that democratic governance has become an established international norm over the last twenty-five years. However, the precise degree of impact that U.S. democracy promotion has had on this trend is unclear.

Democracy promotion, defined as efforts to support the ability of people to strengthen democracy in their home country, has long been supported by U.S. leaders and the public as a U.S. foreign policy objective. Public support has recently declined, however, due to the Bush administration's rhetorical conflation of the U.S. military invasion of Iraq with democracy promotion. Extreme partisan division has also contributed to the recent decrease in the U.S. public's support for the policy. A recent poll by conducted by the German Marshall Fund found that only 45 percent of Americans support

---

10. See Puddington, "Freedom in the World," http://65.110.85.181/upload/pdf/essay2006.pdf.

democracy promotion, down from 52 percent the year before.[11] Support for democracy promotion has strengthened in Europe. When asked whether it should be the role of the European Union to help establish democracy in other countries, 71 percent of Europeans agreed, while a substantial majority opposed the use of force to promote democracy.[12]

The purpose of the September 6 meeting was to assess the status of the U.S. policy of democracy promotion, specifically addressing U.S. perceptions of democracy, conditions under which the United States can successfully promote democracy, regional challenges that inhibit democracy promotion, and potential surprise scenarios that may result in a reversal of this trend.

I. SUMMARY

Despite democracy's solid record of advancement, many participants were troubled by the state of U.S. democracy promotion. Several group members cautioned that U.S.' idealistic perception of democracy as a morally universal goal is not always shared, especially in regions such as Africa, Southeast Asia, and the Middle East. Democracy is often perceived by others more instrumentally as a tool to achieve objectives such as social justice or the redistribution of wealth and less as an intrinsically superior system of governance. Democracy and its promotion also face formidable challenges in Latin America, Africa, and Southeast Asia.

Nonetheless, this state of affairs did not argue for retreating from supporting the spread of democracy. Several group members argued that promoting freedom and democracy in the world reflects the values that have made the United States great and advances key national security interests in the long term. They contended that convergence of all U.S. interests in the short term is never assured, but democratic governments are more likely than autocracies to promote international prosperity and stability.

---

11. See the German Marshall Fund, "Transatlantic Trends 2006," http://www.transatlantictrends.org/doc/2006_TT_Key%20Findings%20-FINAL.pdf.

12. Ibid.

Participants also stressed the importance of determined and skillful U.S. democracy promotion in order to combat the rise of a countermovement lead by Russia and China: By aligning with other autocracies, both powers are pushing back and are threatening to regain influence, to some degree, on the issues of democracy, governance standards, and external interference in internal affairs. This development could emerge as the greatest potential strategic surprise identified by the working group's series on democracy.

II. DEMOCRACY, DEMOCRACY PROMOTION, FREEDOM, AND DEMOCRATIZATION

A number of participants argued that Americans have a deep ideological bias toward viewing democracy as the ultimate end state. Embedded in this understanding are a number of cultural values and principles rooted in U.S. constitutional history. Other societies approach democracy more cynically. To these societies, democracy is not the ultimate end state but merely another means of governing. Group members agreed that democracy is both a means and an end, but this nuanced interpretation often hinders U.S. democracy promotion in places like Southeast Asia, Africa, and the Middle East.

The U.S. perception of democracy has shaped its democracy promotion rhetoric and strategies. It has molded successful programs and bureaucracies such as the U.S. Agency for International Development (USAID), Radio Free Europe/Asia, the Millennium Challenge Corporation, and the National Endowment for Democracy. The hallmark of these programs is that they are designed to assist domestic groups in other countries that are pressing for democratic transformation and consolidation. The Bush administration has elevated the place of democracy promotion in U.S. foreign policy and added to the list of programs. Nevertheless, some members noted that the administration's freedom agenda rhetoric and its conflation of regime change and democracy assistance has undermined the reputation of the U.S. commitment to democracy promotion. In this regard, it is worth noting that the United States sometimes uses democracy promotion as a "weapon" brought to bear on hostile governments and not as a program to be entered into with friendly regimes. As evidence, some members cited the administration's inconsistency of approach: in Egypt and Saudi Arabia, it has made some efforts toward encouraging democratic development; in Iran and Syria, the administration uses strident rhetoric and overt pressure. The administration has also been accused of inconsistency in its support of democratic means but resistive to democratic results, as for example when Palestinian elections brought Hamas to power. Other participants discussed inconsistencies between the U.S. policies of democracy promotion and the Global War on Terror. In Pakistan, for example, the United States is sending contrasting messages to an authoritarian regime. There is a risk that the short-term antiterrorism goals will transfer skills to autocratic countries like Pakistan, enabling them to delay or impede democratization.

Several group members expressed concern over sending mixed messages on democracy. Internationally, autocrats have fostered opposition to the Bush administration's rhetoric in an effort to tarnish the democracy promotion agenda. Domestically, Congress and the U.S. public are now debating the merits of democracy promotion. During a 2006 hearing before the House International Relations Committee, Rep. Henry Hyde (R-IL) argued that "it [democracy] is an uncontrollable experiment with an outcome akin to that faced by the Sorcerer's Apprentice."[13]

The current tendency to equate democracy and freedom is questionable: While it is true that there needs to be a certain degree of freedom for democracy to develop, several members argued that freedom does not always ensure democracy. In addition to freedom, democracy requires a complex political system with strong institutions, the rule of law, freedom of expression, and a credible opposition.

Another challenge facing democracy promotion policymakers is the difficulty of recognizing democratization as it is occurring. Democratization is the critical process a country undergoes to get to the end state of democracy. In the early stages of a country's transition, policymakers have a difficult time differentiating between whether or not the change is a genuine democratic shift or simply a hiatus between two authoritarian or semi-authoritarian regimes.

---

13. House Committee on International Relations, *The International Affairs Budget Request for Fiscal Year 2007*, Henry Hyde's opening statement, 109th Cong., 2nd Sess., February 26, 2006.

III. WHEN AND WHERE TO USE DEMOCRACY PROMOTION

Another challenge to the U.S. policy of democracy promotion is knowing when and where effectively to use democracy promotion. Participants were generally opposed to the notion of using force to promote democracy. They argued that historically the United States has used force to overthrow brutal regimes or totalitarian adversaries, thereby creating the potential for a democratic government to emerge, but that it has not tended to invade another country with the initial primary purpose of installing a democratic government.

Group members also contended that promoting democracy in postconflict environments or inherently unstable or weak states is problematic because of a lack of security. In other words, it is difficult to promote democratic change if citizens do not enjoy some minimum level of security. A number of participants pointed out that this dilemma underscores the importance of persuading the security community in a country where the United States is promoting democracy that a democratic transition is both desirable and in their interest. It is not enough to support just civil society agents; the United States also has to nudge the coercive instruments of the state to buy into the long-term prospects of democracy. For example, in Indonesia the democratic transition did not take hold until military leaders like President Yudhoyono agreed that it was in the country's best interest to change. Moreover, in Nigeria, General Atiku Abubakar's decision to remove the military from the government was critical to its democratic transition.

IV. REGIONAL CHALLENGES

Challenges in Latin America, Africa, and Southeast Asia

Throughout the series, participants explored the obstacles to democratic consolidation in Latin America, Africa, and Southeast Asia, as well as the hurdles facing U.S. democracy promotion efforts. All three regions continue to suffer from weak institutions; underdeveloped political party structures; limits on opposition movements; corruption; and, in some cases, popular demagoguery. In all three regions, the largest and most significant powers (Brazil, Nigeria, South Africa, and Indonesia) do not always wield their influence in a manner that affects the democratic development of their neighbors in a positive way, nor is it certain that smaller democratic states have the ability to be regional democratic leaders. The three regions also share the risk of becoming "hijacked" democracies to the degree that (a) long-time incumbents and in some cases new arrivals (Chávez) are in a position to stack the political deck and manipulate electoral politicking and/or (b) "people power" movements organize "the street" to force their will upon weak, elected governments that lose touch with their societies.

Group members also pointed out region-specific challenges. Economic trends differ substantially in each region. Socioeconomic inequality emerges as a critical and salient challenge with particular vehemence in Latin America. Incumbent leaders are subjected to the rigors of "performance legitimacy" tests to a greater extent in Southeast Asia and Latin America; African polities generally appear less respectful of term limits and more responsive to external, donor pressures than to the demands of their own domestic societies. Africa's relative dependence makes it more vulnerable to western pro-democracy pressures, though this is declining due to the Russia/China factor. The "demonstration effect" of events in one country impacting trends elsewhere in the region is most pronounced in Latin America and Africa, but much less so in Southeast Asia due to differentiating and buffering circumstances. Southeast Asia and Africa still suffer from a substantial number of autocratic regimes. Fortunately, Latin America is only plagued by one true autocracy (Cuba).

Challenges in the Middle East

During the final meeting, group members turned to consider some of the challenges to U.S. democracy promotion in the Middle East, not the least of which is the deep popular antipathy to U.S. policies in the region. There was little support for the conventional wisdom that Islam somehow inhibits the indigenous promotion of democracy and democratic values. There are many important changes taking place in the Middle East that may have little to do with U.S. democracy promotion efforts or rhetoric. Interestingly, these changes are often developing within the Islamist movement. The liberal secularist parties that the United States traditionally supported are so politically weakened that they can no longer effectively press for democratic transition or hold off Islamist advances. However, it is possible that the current shift in the Islamist movement may be the early stages of democratization. According to one expert, Islamist parties are dividing themselves into religious and political organizations. The religious dimension is designed to appeal to the portion of their base that is committed to a certain set of values, while the political entity is designed to give the party the flexibility to be pragmatic enough to govern effectively. Some members argued that a certain degree of pluralism is forming in the Islamist movement. Like all political parties, the new Islamist parties will compete with each other, and they will have to perform in order to maintain influence.

Despite the changes occurring in the Middle East's Islamist movement, other group members were less optimistic. They contended that it is too early to determine whether or not these shifts are a sign of democratization. Overall, they were discouraged with the results of democratic elections held in Palestine, the recent events in Lebanon, the inability of the democratically elected Iraqi government to quell secular violence, and the prevailing number of entrenched autocracies present in the region.

Strategic Surprise

Of most concern to members of the working group is the rise of a palpable antidemocratic undertow at the multilateral level led by Russia and China. In Latin America, Africa, Southeast Asia, and the Middle East, Russia and China are increasing their influence by acquiring natural resource assets, often outbidding western competitors, and providing soft loans to egregious regimes. Such policies may provide an alternative source of support for autocracies that chafe under western pressure for democratic reform. Domestically, Russia has enacted heightened controls on local and foreign NGOs, and China has recently condemned the U.S.' "democratic offensive" as self-serving, coercive, and immoral. The Chinese Communist Party reportedly has also mapped out a strategy for resisting U.S. and European efforts to promote so-called "color revolutions" in China and its neighborhood.

Evidence that the backlash has become widespread can be found in Uzbekistan, Kazakhstan, Tajikistan, and Belarus. Following the example set by Russia and China, autocratic leaders in these countries are in the process of shutting down most of the western democracy programs, as well as most of the domestic NGOs that work on democracy issues. In Africa, Zimbabwe's President Robert

Mugabe has driven out western NGOs and forced the closure of many local groups that get external support. Ethiopia expelled the IRI (International Republican Institute) and the NDI (National Democratic Institute) prior to its 2005 elections, and Eritrea requested that USAID cease operations in the country, stating that it was uncomfortable with the agency's activities, which include promoting citizen participation in political life. In South America, Venezuelan President Hugo Chávez regularly blasts U.S. democracy promotion as being part of the Bush administration's campaign to oust him.

More disturbingly, Russia and China are rallying support to resist democracy promotion, taking advantage of the fundamental rift triggered by the close association of democracy promotion with U.S. military intervention in the Middle East. Leaders in both countries are seeking a return to an international system where sovereignty prevails over humanitarian crises and freedom and where the international norm is not to interfere in the domestic affairs of others. At the UN Security Council, both countries are working with some degree of collaboration to protect Iran, North Korea, and Sudan. In the UN Human Rights Council, China and Russia, along with the Organization of the Islamic Conference, have sponsored resolutions defending the right of religious leaders in countries to make blasphemous statements they disagree with. Both countries also supported Venezuela's bid for a seat on the UN Security Council, a position Chávez hoped to use as a bully pulpit to attack the United States and foil resolutions aimed at his allies, including North Korea, Iran, and Cuba.

Though this antidemocratic pole has yet to fully develop, it has gained enough momentum to threaten the global expansion and consolidation of democracy. Unless the United States is able to regain international credibility in terms of democracy promotion, there is potential for a global retreat from the current preferential trend for democratic governance.

Policy Implications

Participants generally concluded that democracy promotion should remain a priority in U.S. foreign policy. However, they argued that the present U.S. rhetoric and methods used to promote democracy fall short of the strategy required to deal with current challenges. A new strategy needs to be developed that looks through what are inevitably going to be unstable transitions and setbacks. For example, when a country elects a group like Hamas, several participants argued that the United States should bear in mind that experience in other countries suggests that the pressures of governing may lead to the moderation and evolution of the more extremist elements of the party. Though this outcome is not always guaranteed, there could be other benefits, as Fareed Zakaria suggests: "If politics is more open, these groups may or may not moderate themselves, but they will surely lose some of the mystical allure they now have. The martyrs will become mayors, which is quite a fall in status."[14]

Participants argued that the strategy will require all elements of the U.S. government. In addition to USAID and the Millennium Challenge Corporation, the Central Intelligence Agency, the Department of Justice, and the Department of Defense also have roles to play in the strategy. For example, by conducting joint training operations with friendly autocracies, these agencies have access to the security forces that are so critical to democratic reform. Members argued that during these training operations the United States may be able to influence their perceptions toward a democratic transition.

Other group members contended that this strategy must also be seen as a multilateral endeavor. The polls have shown that our allies support democracy promotion, but that they will not support using force in an effort to do so. Another way to increase multilateral support is to show that the United States is committed to democracy promotion as a matter of principle by acting with a modicum of consistency. In addition to pressuring enemy regimes, America must apply steady pressure to friendly autocracies. Group members argued that more consistency is also needed to synchronize the level of rhetoric and budget support for democracy promotion in Africa, Southeast Asia, and the Middle East. Finally, the U.S. government can help support long-term institution building by assisting U.S. nongovernmental organizations like the National Democratic Institute, the International Republican Institute, and the Asia Foundation that operate privately but utilize public money.

In the end, the session concluded that fighting dictatorship and the antidemocratic backlash will require a subtle diplomatic hand. In some cases, pushing back hard may get results; in others, it may only fuel nationalist sentiments. The U.S. policy of democracy promotion

---

14. See Fareed Zakaria, "Islam and Power," *Newsweek* (international ed.), February 13, 2006, p. 34.

must be consistent and patient. Aid must be directed toward improving the homegrown institutional capacity programs, anticorruption initiatives, political pluralism forums, and human rights agendas in countries undergoing democratic transition and/or consolidation. To be successful against the sources of the democracy backlash, the United States must work with other democracies to coordinate their efforts to reclaim the initiative from Russia and China, and Iran and Venezuela, which too often oppose U.S. efforts to foster political pluralism.

Schlesinger Working Group Core Members

Below are the core members of the Schlesinger Working Group, though not all members participated in this series. Core members of the Schlesinger Working Group were not asked to approve this Report, although the Report relies heavily on the discussions of the group. As such, this document reflects the general ideas of working group members but is not a consensus document and cannot be ascribed to any individual member.

Morton I. Abramowitz
Elliott Abrams
Pauline Baker
Nancy Bearg
Hans Binnendijk
Thomas Boyatt
Michael E. Brown
Chester A. Crocker
Chas Freeman
Francis Fukuyama
Robert L. Gallucci
Toby Gati
H. Allen Holmes
James Jones
Farooq Kathwari
Geoffrey Kemp
Richard Kerr
Ellen Laipson
Samuel W. Lewis
Princeton Lyman
Wallace Mathai-Davis

Jessica T. Mathews
Charles William Maynes
Robert C. McFarlane
Donald McHenry
Moisés Naím
William L. Nash
Phyllis Oakley
Robert Oakley
William Odom
Stephen Rosenfeld
Howard B. Schaffer
Teresita Schaffer
James R. Schlesinger
Brent Scowcroft
Richard Solomon
Tara Sonenshine
Helmut Sonnenfeldt
Paul Stares
Robert Sutter
Frank G. Wisner
Casimir A. Yost

About the Author

Sara Thannhauser is the program officer for the Schlesinger Working Group at Georgetown University's Institute for the Study of Diplomacy. Ms. Thannhauser has previously worked as a research assistant at the State Department's Foreign Service Institute, Crisis Management Training Center. She has also worked for the Justice Department's Office of International Affairs, Criminal Division.

Ms. Thannhauser holds a master's degree in International Affairs from American University's School of International Service and an undergraduate degree in political science from Saint Bonaventure University.